AWESOME ATHLETES

MICHELLE WIE

Jill C. Wheeler

ABDO Publishing Company

visit us at
www.abdopublishing.com

Published by ABDO Publishing Company, 4940 Viking Drive, Edina, Minnesota 55435.
Copyright © 2007 by Abdo Consulting Group, Inc. International copyrights reserved in all
countries. No part of this book may be reproduced in any form without written permission from
the publisher. The Checkerboard Library™ is a trademark and logo of ABDO Publishing
Company.

Printed in the United States.

Cover Photo: Corbis
Interior Photos: AP/Wide World pp. 5, 8, 13, 16, 19, 21, 23, 24, 27, 28-29; Corbis pp. 6, 7, 9, 10,
    11, 14, 15, 17, 25; Getty Images pp. 16, 26; Robert Beck/Sports Illustrated p. 18

Series Coordinator: Rochelle Baltzer
Editors: Rochelle Baltzer, Heidi M. Dahmes
Art Direction: Neil Klinepier

Library of Congress Cataloging-in-Publication Data

Wheeler, Jill C., 1964-
  Michelle Wie / Jill C. Wheeler.
      p. cm. -- (Awesome athletes)
  Includes index.
  ISBN-10 1-59928-309-3
  ISBN-13 978-1-59928-309-8
  1. Wie, Michelle--Juvenile literature. 2. Golfers--United States--Biography--Juvenile literature.
3. Women golfers--United States--Biography--Juvenile literature. I. Title. II. Series.

  GV964.W49W46 2007
  796.352092--dc22
                                                                    2006000577

Contents

Michelle Wie 4

Only Child 6

Big Hitter 8

On to Tournaments 10

Young Champion 12

The Making of an Awesome Athlete 16

Teen Sensation 18

PGA Qualifier 20

Turning Pro 22

Wie Today 26

Glossary 30

Web Sites 31

Index 32

Michelle Wie

Michelle Wie is one of the youngest, most talented golfers today. At 16, she became the world's highest-paid female golfer in history. Most golf stars Wie's age compete against amateurs. Yet, this teenager takes on professional women and men alike.

Wie's golf swing is nearly perfect. She is known for her long, consistent **drives**. She claims her career-best drive is 391 yards (358 m). This is farther than most men can hit. But most important, Wie hits solid drives time after time.

With her outstanding talent, Wie has earned a faithful following. When she competes, television ratings and ticket sales increase an average of 50 percent! Wie adds excitement to the game of golf. Like her hero, professional golfer Tiger Woods, Wie attracts new fans to an old game.

Opposite Page: Wie's power has brought her much success on and off the course. She has already been a guest on popular talk shows and has appeared in countless magazines. She has even golfed with former president Bill Clinton!

Only Child

Michelle Sung Wie was born on October 11, 1989, in Honolulu, Hawaii. She is the only child of Byung-Wook "B.J." and Hyun Kyong "Bo" Wie. B.J. is a professor at the University of Hawaii. Bo is a **real estate** agent.

Honolulu is the capital city of Hawaii, and it has a population of 371,657.

Both B.J. and Bo were born in South Korea and later moved to the United States. The two married in California in 1988. Eventually, they moved to Honolulu.

Sports have always been important to the Wies. Back in South Korea, Bo's golf game had featured long, powerful **drives**. She had even won the Korean Women's Amateur tournament!

Bo taught her family to play golf. Michelle swung her first golf club at just four years old. B.J. recalls his daughter could drive the ball more than 100 yards (91 m)!

In addition to golf, Michelle played soccer, softball, and tennis. By the time she was seven, her parents noticed she played golf and tennis best. So, they encouraged her to focus on those two sports. However, Michelle did not like to run. So, she eventually gave up on tennis and worked on her golfing abilities.

Michelle was a bright child and did well in school. She did not let her success on the golf course interfere with studying.

Big Hitter

Soon, B.J. and Bo realized Michelle had inherited her mother's talent for golf. However, Michelle needed practice. She enjoyed hitting the ball hard. But, she did not care much which direction it went. So, B.J. and Bo helped Michelle improve her aim. They worked with her to copy Tiger Woods's swing.

Tiger Woods excelled at golf at a young age, just like Michelle!

Michelle's promise as a golfer was starting to become clear. At seven, she was **driving** the ball much farther than other children her age, including boys. Michelle's power amazed others.

At eight, Michelle began beating her parents at golf. The next year, both B.J. and Bo put away their golf clubs. They decided to spend their time helping Michelle improve her game. Sometimes, that task required creativity. To inspire Michelle, B.J. and Bo put posters of Tiger Woods around their house.

As Michelle improved, her parents started talking with her about competing in golf tournaments. Tournaments are exciting. Yet practicing for them can become boring. Sometimes, Michelle had to practice the same hit 100 times! So, B.J. and Bo used money to help encourage her. They paid her 25¢ each time she made **par** on a hole.

Michelle's parents also arranged their work schedules to fit Michelle's practices. At least one, if not both, of them worked with her every day.

The Wies are a close family. Michelle admits that she probably wouldn't practice as much if her mother was not on the golf course with her.

9

On to Tournaments

Michelle played her first tournament in 1999. She led the course until the last two holes. Then, she hit three shots into the water on the second-to-last hole. She **putted** four times on the final hole, resulting in a tie. She had to win a **chip**-off, or tiebreaker, to win the tournament. Fortunately, she chipped the ball three inches (8 cm) from the hole for a victory!

When Michelle first started playing golf, B.J. was her caddie. He carried Michelle's golf clubs and assisted her on the course.

In 2000, Michelle became the youngest player to qualify for **match play** at the U.S. Women's Amateur Public Links Championship. This was Michelle's first experience playing in a serious competition. She played well but lost in the first round.

Soon after the championship, Michelle received a request to appear on *The Tonight Show with Jay Leno*. However, B.J. turned it down. That week, Michelle would be entering sixth grade at a new school. Her father wanted her to have a good start at Punahou School with no distractions.

Punahou School is considered one of Hawaii's best private schools. Its 3,700 students range from kindergarten through grade 12.

Young Champion

Michelle quickly settled into a new schedule at Punahou. After school on weekdays, her parents took her to a local golf course. There, Michelle practiced at least three hours. On weekends, she put in another seven to eight hours each day.

Sometimes, practice was tiresome. B.J. and Bo videotaped Michelle's shots. Then, they reviewed them to determine what she could do better. Often, Michelle had to practice something repeatedly until she got it right.

In 2001, Michelle's hard work paid off. In May, she won the Jennie K. Wilson Invitational by nine strokes. This competition is the most highly regarded women's golf tournament in Hawaii. At 11, Michelle was the youngest to ever win the event!

Michelle played in her second U.S. Women's Amateur Public Links Championship in June. This time, she made it to the third round of **match play**. Then in August, Michelle became the youngest to win the Hawaii State Women's Golf Association **Stroke Play** Championship.

Opposite Page: **Michelle claims that if she ever feels bored with golf, she'll start over and play left-handed.**

In 2002, Michelle continued to improve her record. At 12, she became the youngest player to **Monday qualify** for a **Ladies Professional Golf Association (LPGA)** tournament. Her score in qualifying play allowed her to compete in the Takefuji Classic in March.

In May, Michelle's parents traveled with her to Bradenton, Florida. There, Michelle attended the David Leadbetter Junior Golf Academy.

At the academy, Michelle worked with swing coach Gary Gilchrist. Michelle's abilities impressed Gilchrist. He said she had more potential than any other girl he'd ever seen. Michelle returned to the academy twice more that year.

Gilchrist continued to work with Michelle through 2004. He focused on improving her short game, including putts and chips.

At 12, Michelle stood nearly six feet (2 m) tall! She says her height helps her see farther on the golf course.

In June, Michelle played in her third U.S. Women's Amateur Public Links Championship. This time, she advanced to the semifinals! Michelle became the youngest semifinalist in the event's history. And in November, Michelle won the women's division of the Hawaii State Open by a whopping 13 strokes!

Michelle Wie is one of the most exciting golfers today. Like Tiger Woods, she refreshes the game and gives it a more cool, athletic image.

1989	1994	1999	2000
Born on October 11 in Honolulu, Hawaii	Begins playing golf at age four	Plays in her first tournament	Becomes the youngest player to qualify for match play at the U.S. Women's Amateur Public Links Championship

How Awesome Is She?

Wie routinely drives balls 300 yards (274 m). Her powerful drives bring her success in tournaments. In 2003, Wie became the youngest to win the U.S. Women's Amateur Public Links Championship. Today, she still holds this place.

Golfer	Age	Year Won
Michelle Wie	**13**	**2003**
Ya-Ni Tseng	15	2004
Catherine Cartwright	17	2000
Eun Jung Lee	17	2005

MICHELLE WIE

PROFESSIONAL TOURNAMENT WINS: 1
SWINGS: RIGHT-HANDED
HEIGHT: 6 FEET
WEIGHT: 150 POUNDS

2001	**2002**	**2003**	**2005**
Wins Jennie K. Wilson Invitational	Plays at LPGA Takefuji Classic	Wins U.S. Women's Amateur Public Links Championship	Turns professional

- Shot a low score of 64 at age ten

- Became the first woman to qualify for an adult men's U.S. Golf Association championship

- Appearance in the 2005 U.S. Women's Open helped to set a record for the highest number of ESPN viewers watching a women's golf event

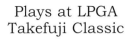

Teen Sensation

Michelle found even more success in 2003. At just 13, she played against some of the world's best golfers. Many of those golfers were grown men.

In January, Michelle made headlines. She attempted to qualify for the **Professional Golfers' Association (PGA)** Sony Open. Michelle was the only female in the lineup. Unfortunately, she did not make the **cut**.

Michelle attracts attention wherever she plays.

Days later, she played an **exhibition** round at a local country club. Her partner was PGA professional Jerry Kelly. Michelle outgunned him with several shots on the practice range. When the exhibition ended, Kelly asked Michelle for her **autograph**!

In March, Michelle played in the Kraft Nabisco Championship. This was her first **major**. Michelle turned heads with her 280-yard (256-m) **drives**. She ended the competition tied for ninth place.

In June, Michelle made her fourth appearance at the U.S. Women's Amateur Public Links Championship. This time she was victorious! She became the youngest golfer to ever win the event.

At 13, Michelle became the youngest winner in the 108-year history of U.S. Golf Association adult championships.

PGA Qualifier

Some people in the golf world had grumbled when Michelle tried to qualify for the 2003 Sony Open. They said she was too young. And, they thought she had no business playing golf with grown men. Yet Michelle was determined to compete against both women and men.

The following year, there was more griping when Michelle returned to the event. But this time, she qualified! Michelle became the youngest person, and only the fourth female, to play in a **PGA** Tour tournament. However, she missed the second-round **cut** by just one stroke. Still, her **drives** averaged 271 yards (248 m).

In summer 2004, Michelle played in the qualifying rounds for the U.S. Amateur Public Links Championship. Traditionally, the winner of that event is invited to play in the Masters Tournament. That meant 14-year-old Michelle had a shot at the biggest win in golf! No woman has ever played in the Masters.

Michelle was the only woman on the course for the qualifying rounds. She took third place, finishing just

In July, Michelle and 17-year-old Paula Creamer tied for the top amateur place in the U.S. Women's Open.

two strokes away from being able to compete in the championship. Therefore, she also lost her chance to play in the Masters.

Turning Pro

In January 2005, Michelle played in the Sony Open once more. Unfortunately, she performed worse than the previous year. She missed the second-round **cut** by seven strokes.

However, Michelle proved her place in professional events that summer. She made it to the quarterfinals at the U.S. Amateur Public Links Championship! Then, she was defeated by 20-year-old Clay Ogden.

Later that year, Michelle's **status** in the golf world advanced. Just five days before her sixteenth birthday, Michelle announced she was turning professional. This meant that she could start accepting money for performance in tournaments.

Michelle cannot officially join the **LPGA** Tour until she is 18. However, **sponsors** allow golfers to play in professional events in exchange for promoting their brand. The LPGA allows six of such instances per year.

Shortly after her announcement, Michelle signed contracts with Sony and Nike. At $10 to 12 million annually, these contracts made her the highest-paid female golfer in history!

Opposite Page: Even before Michelle signed with Nike, she wore the brand on the course. At the 2005 U.S. Amateur Public Links, she sported a Nike belt.

To manage Michelle's professional golf career, the Wies hired the William Morris Agency. This talent agency aims to make Michelle a worldwide golf star. Fashion experts help her choose stylish clothes. And, they teach her how to fix her hair and makeup. Michelle even gets lessons on how to move while being filmed.

Michelle's first professional appearance was on October 13 at the Samsung World Championship. She began strong but was disqualified during the third round.

LPGA rules officials said Michelle had taken an illegal **drop**. They claimed the ball was placed closer to the hole than it should have been. Michelle had not realized the error. As a result, she missed out on $53,126 in prize money.

Michelle shares a laugh with LPGA professional Cristie Kerr. The two have played practice rounds together since Michelle was 13.

In spring 2006, Michelle made important breakthroughs. She tied for third place at the Kraft Nabisco Championship. This was her first **major** as a professional.

Then, Michelle made her first men's

Michelle earned more than $100,000 at the 2006 Kraft Nabisco Championship. Yet much of her earnings goes into a special fund that she can't access until she is an adult.

professional **cut** at the SK Telecom Open in South Korea. She became only the second female to make a cut in a Korean men's professional tournament.

Michelle's success continued into summer. In June, she tied for fifth place at the LPGA Championship. Then in July, Michelle tied for third place at the U.S. Women's Open.

Wie Today

Today, golf and high school continue to fill Wie's schedule. But in her free time, Wie likes to read and draw. She is a fan of the Harry Potter series. Wie also enjoys watching movies and shopping with her friends.

Like many teenagers, Wie worries about getting into college. She thinks professional athletes need a college education to help them make smart decisions. Currently, Wie's top college choice is Stanford University in California. This is also where Tiger Woods attended school. Wie plans to study business or finance.

In the meantime, Wie has plenty of pressures to handle. Some people say she has not won enough tournaments to justify her **status**. Her most recent tournament win was in 2003.

A Stanford University stuffed animal key ring hangs from Wie's golf bag.

One day, Wie hopes to play on the **PGA** Tour and win the Masters. So, she continues to improve her golf skills.

Right now, her **drives** capture attention. Yet in the golf world, many games are won or lost near the **putting green**. So, Wie practices **chipping** and **putting**. And, she works with a specialist to improve her mental game. Today, Wie's future looks brighter than ever.

Even professional golfers have room for improvement. Wie continues to work on putts.

Glossary

autograph - a person's handwritten name.

chip - a short golf shot made near the putting green.

cut - a required score to qualify for further play in a golf tournament.

drive - the first shot on a hole at a golf course.

drop - when a golf ball is released by hand to be put back into play. This happens after the ball is declared unplayable.

exhibition - a public showing of athletic skill.

Ladies Professional Golf Association (LPGA) - an organization that promotes women in professional golf.

major - any of four annual grouped tournaments in both the LPGA and the PGA. The LPGA majors are the Kraft Nabisco Championship, the LPGA Championship, the U.S. Women's Open, and the Women's British Open. The PGA majors are the Masters Tournament, the U.S. Open, the British Open, and the PGA Championship.

match play - a golf competition in which the player or the team that wins the most holes is the winner of the competition.

Monday qualify - to qualify to compete in a professional golf tournament on the Monday before it begins by meeting strict standards against many competitive challengers.

par - the standard number of strokes a player should take to complete a hole or a round of golf with a good performance.

Professional Golfers' Association (PGA) - an organization that promotes and regulates the profession of golf.

putt - a light golf stroke made on the putting green.

putting green - the smooth grass or sand around the hole into which a player putts a golf ball.

real estate - property, which includes buildings and land.

sponsor - someone who pays for a program or an activity in return for promotion of a particular product or brand.

status - a position or rank in a social or professional standing.

stroke play - a golf competition in which the total number of strokes determines the winner.

Web Sites

To learn more about Michelle Wie, visit ABDO Publishing Company on the World Wide Web at **www.abdopublishing.com**. Web sites about Wie are featured on our Book Links page. These links are routinely monitored and updated to provide the most current information available.

Index

D
David Leadbetter Junior Golf Academy 14

E
education 10, 12, 26

F
family 6, 7, 8, 9, 10, 12, 14, 24

G
Gilchrist, Gary 14

H
Hawaii State Open 15
Hawaii State Women's Golf Association Stroke Play Championship 12
hobbies 7, 26

J
Jennie K. Wilson Invitational 12

K
Kelly, Jerry 18

M
majors 19, 20, 21, 25, 27

O
Ogden, Clay 22

S
Samsung World Championship 24
SK Telecom Open 25
Sony Open 18, 20, 22
South Korea 6, 25
sponsorships 22

T
Takefuji Classic 14
Tonight Show with Jay Leno, The 10

U
U.S. Amateur Public Links Championship 20, 21, 22
U.S. Women's Amateur Public Links Championship 10, 12, 15, 19

W
William Morris Agency 24
Woods, Tiger 4, 8, 26